MW01093297

The Marriage Meeting Guide

How a Simple 30-Minute Weekly Can
Transform Your Marriage

(A 15-Minute Read—A Lifetime of Benefits)

By Jordan Fowler and Amy Fowler

Printed by Amazon, in the United States of America.

First printing, 2019

Jordan Fowler
11536 Twining Branch Circle
Haslet, TX 76052

https://themarriagemeeting.com

Table of Contents

The Marriage Meeting Introduction

This simple guide to a weekly meeting with your spouse can transform your marriage. Whether you are engaged, are a newlywed, have been married for years, or are re-married, conducting a weekly 30-minute marriage meet-up will improve your marriage more than you can imagine.

Those Who Will Benefit:
- If you have a good marriage and want to make it better.
- If you feel like you and your spouse do not communicate about the most important things.
- If you want to lessen fighting and arguments in your marriage.
- If you feel like your marriage is stuck on cruise control and not growing.
- If you feel distant at times from your spouse, like two ships passing in the night.
- If you are engaged and want to start your marriage healthier than most.

Our Story

Amy and I have both been previously married. We've experienced the horrible pain of divorce and wanted to be more intentional and proactive in our marriage. Before we got married, we received some sound counsel from a wise friend, and what a difference it has made!

Amy as an elementary school counselor is an extrovert. She is very accustomed to discussing challenges and feelings. I, Jordan, am a processing introvert. The natural place for me to sweep feelings and challenges is under the rug, to avoid having to face and deal with them.

Our friend noted that if I, as her introverted husband, didn't take the lead in addressing our relationship, Amy might become resentful in the absence of such leadership.

Your marriage may be inversed where the husband is the extrovert, and the wife is the introvert. Or perhaps, you are both extroverts and love to see the sparks fly, or you are two introverts, and remove yourselves to your respective caves.

Does This Work?

During our years of marriage, Amy and I have had two minor arguments. Why? Because we are so saintly? Hardly. Left to our own devices there would be many more fights. (And life has definitely thrown us our share of challenges.) It's largely a result of the communication skills we have learned and continue to practice during our weekly meetings that help guide our discussions throughout the week. We are able to voice things in ways we are heard, so that emotions and reactions don't escalate.

If you were to ask us to rate our marriage on a scale of 1 to 10, both of us would answer 9.9 because, yes, there is always room for growth. As an outcome of the communication and intimacy fostered through the meeting, it is easy for us to both claim one another as our best friend—Amy thinking I am the best possible husband and me thinking she is the best possible wife!

Regardless of where you are in your marriage, this guide will help you strengthen it.

Scheduling the Meeting

We've found setting an absolute non-wavering time for the meeting works best. So for us, Wednesday is sacred. We guard it as a date night/meeting night, a commitment to one another. In a jokingly way, I, as the husband, call the meeting to order by exclaiming, "Meeting come to order!" It is important to Amy that I take the lead in this effort.

The reason a weekly meeting is powerful is that there is a set time to address positive and negative issues in your marriage. The critique feels less like criticism and doesn't seem to come from left field because the time is scheduled and the framework given.

The meeting length varies: sometimes the meeting is short, and other times, we find ourselves spending additional time talking, enjoying time together.

Where to Have the Meeting

For us, it's facing one another on the couch. We don't want a table or anything between us as we talk as it can feel like a barrier leading to one spouse feeling emotionally closed off. We want to feel connected. We mark this time off as sacred, therefore; we don't allow distractions from kids, texts, television, or phone calls.

Why Questions and Not Just Chatting

Having key questions in place ensures we talk about what matters most to the health of a marriage. Yes, we also chat during our meetings but only after we've dealt with the fundamental questions that help us communicate about the vital aspects of a successful marriage.

Now, on to the simple meeting questions agenda....

Weekly Meeting Questions

We will explain the significance of each question on the following pages. You can use this page as a simple guide, week after week. Both husband and wife need to be willing to communicate and actively listen for this to be beneficial.

1. How have I met or exceeded your expectations this week?

2. How did I not meet your expectations or need to improve at meeting them?

3. How do you feel about our spiritual intimacy?

4. How do you feel about our finances?

5. How do you feel about our physical intimacy?

6. How do you feel about your job? How do you feel about my job?

7. Is there anything you are struggling with or stressed about? How can I help?

If You Have Kids

8. What parenting skills have you seen as positive? Are there areas that need improvement?

9. Do you have any concerns about the kids?

Others

10. Is there any way you have seen me treat others that I should be aware of? If yes, what is a better way of handling the situation?

The Significance of Each Question

To use a boxing metaphor, we have found these questions keep us in the same corner rather than seeing each other as opponents. Remember, the meeting's purpose is not to attack or vent but to build intimacy. Remind yourselves you are in one another's corner; you are a team and a helpmate for one another. You are doing this exercise, not to break the other's spirit, but to build one another up and to create a stronger marriage.

Within the next section, we outlined the importance of each question. You don't have to look at these pages for every meeting, but you will want to read this section together before your *first* meeting.

Expectation Questions

Question 1

Positive Expectations

Praising our spouse for meeting an expectation is the single best way to get them to repeat that process. This is why this is question #1! It starts your time together in a positive way.

Example: Honey, I really appreciated it this week when you _____.
Example: Do you remember how we talked last week about how I'd like you to _____?
You really did a much better job on that. Thank you.

Question 2

Unmet Expectations

Our expectations drive our assumptions.

Example: My dad took the trash out for my mom weekly, so I, the wife, assume you, the husband will, too, while the husband grew up in a home where whoever saw the trash can full took it out.

Example: When I texted you about how bad a day I was having, you didn't acknowledge it with any kind of response. I'd appreciate it if you could simply even text back, "Sorry babe. I hope it gets better."

These expectations may seem reasonable to you; however, your spouse might have a different background and set of assumptions.

Bobb Biehl, a renowned life coach, says nearly all conflicts come from two different sets of assumptions. Think about the last argument you had with your spouse. When you boil it down, it probably resulted from two divergent expectations and assumptions.

When our expectations don't get addressed, internal conflict and tension start boiling inside of us. We begin to think, "How can he/she not know this is important to me?" These unmet expectations can fester and cause explosive arguments over small things that have accumulated. Of course, there are significant unmet expectations that must be addressed, as well. Weekly meetings allow us to get these expectations out on the table.

Once an expectation is revealed, there are only three positive solutions:

1. For one spouse to work to meet the other's expectations.
2. For the expectation giver to modify their expectations with their partner.
3. For the expectation giver to release their expectation in an act of surrendering it.

Some expectations are very reasonable. The expectation giver and receiver can talk about how they would like the expectation fulfilled.

Some expectations are not quite so fair or reasonable. In this case, the expectation needs to be dissected.

A great follow-up question is: Why is this expectation important for you?

Sometimes, you'll find the spouse is bringing something from their past into the present. Other times, fear might be driving the expectation or a feeling of not being cherished, etc. (For example, putting phones away at 8pm and only answering for emergencies is very important for Amy to feel important and cherished.)

If an expectation seems unfair, it is important as a team to get the person to express the motivation behind the expectation. Once they put THE WHY of the expectation into words, you can both work on having them either release the expectation or modifying it into something that is workable. Often, a creative team approach can come up with a concrete solution that meets THE WHY behind the expectation in a way one spouse was not able to see it on their own.

Intimacy Questions

I once heard a wise teacher named Dr. Kitchens say, "Intimacy means 'in-to-me-see.'" When we hide or obscure parts of ourselves, it reduces the quality of our marriage. Allowing your spouse to see into you will foster incredible, healthy intimacy on many levels.

Question 3

Spiritual Intimacy

Being connected spiritually is foundational to a successful marriage. We highly recommend praying together, doing a devotional together and serving together in a local church. Also talking about what God is teaching you in life is important.

If you are not a Christian, you can skip this question. Just know, to Amy and I, it isn't an add-on. It is core to the success of our marriage. We wouldn't make it without our spiritual intimacy with Jesus Christ and one another.

Question 4

Financial Intimacy

Finances are often a big argument point in relationships. One spouse might not feel the other is including them on important financial decisions, or they may think their spouse is hiding something from them.

Discussing how confident you feel about your financial footing builds intimacy. It creates a one-flesh approach to handling your money and resources.

Question 5

Physical Intimacy

Sex and physical touch is vital to a marriage. It is the physical way we experience seeing into one other as we share something special.

Expectations for intimacy can be very different. Often, one spouse's love language of physical touch may be way higher on the list of importance than the other spouse's. As couples, we need to discuss the frequency and quality of physical intimacy in the weekly meeting. Physical intimacy simply means activities that encourage physical closeness and does not always entail sex. There are many ways to show physical intimacy such as holding one another, cuddling, handholding, etc. Physical intimacy will often follow the meeting because of the deepening connection that has occurred.

Talk about your physical intimacy openly and honestly.

Life Situation Questions

Question 6

Work Feelings

Typically, at least one spouse works. Often, they spend a large amount of time at their place of work. We often assume the other spouse can read our minds in regards to how our work life is going.

Make sure this question isn't merely addressing recent happenings, though those are quite welcome. You want to get to the engine room of their heart. What are their joys, fears, concerns and other emotions concerning their work environment? Are they feeling satisfied in their vocation? How do you feel about your spouse's work? Do you see it fulfilling them or draining them?

Question 7

Struggles and Stressors

One way to ensure you are a helpmate for one another is to help carry each other's burdens, struggles, and stressors. It lets us know how to encourage one another.

The second part of the question is vital, as we often rush to say, "Well here is how I would handle that." We give solutions before we hear what our spouse really needs in terms of assistance. By hearing them answer both parts of this question, we can best meet this need and be truly helpful.

Relating to Others (Kids & Friends, Family, Acquaintances)

Feel free to skip question 8 and 9 in this section if you are not parents (or replace kids with grandkids, etc.).

Question 8

Parenting

Our spouses make us better parents. They can see things in our parenting styles and actions that we cannot see. Always try to lead first with the positive in answering this question.

This is a great time to talk about patience, as well as shaping your kid's hearts and actions.

Question 9

Kid's Concerns

This question deals less with parenting but can lead back to it. Maybe you are seeing one of your children withdrawing, struggling, or making poor choices? Perhaps, they have been upset recently. This question allows you to get on the same page and to see if you both are seeing similar characteristics and behaviors. Then an action plan for parenting can be developed as a follow-up.

Question 10

Relating to Others

Our spouse knows us better than anyone else. Why wouldn't I want to tap into that insight to help foster my other relationships? I am introvert and can drift into my own world easily, even sometimes while talking with you face-to-face.

In a few of our meetings, Amy has graciously pointed out that I drifted off in the middle of a conversation with someone (She's a great conversationalist). She'll also tell me the times I handled a challenging person well.

I've been able to speak to her about not writing off someone quickly or assigning motive to someone who has offended her because neither of us knows their backstory.

Frequently Asked Questions

From Amy

The question I always get first: **Do you really wait all week to tell Jordan you are mad about something?** The answer is, of course not.

Some frustrations have to be dealt with immediately. On the other hand, as we have mastered the skill of our meetings, I am *much* more apt to think to myself, "Is this super important or can it wait?" More times than not, I can absolutely wait until our meeting, when I am more calm to express my frustrations and expectations. In turn, I feel like this "wait time" grows me more and more in the area of self-control and patience as the years pass.

The next objection sounds like this: **We've been married so long, my husband would *never* have a meeting with me each week**. I agree that this is counterintuitive for most men, but give it a try! Once he figures out the meetings are not a "beat-down," he will be more than happy to lead them.

From Jordan

I hear men state, **"I feel like I'll just get attacked. How do you keep that from happening?"**

Start each meeting reminding one another that the purpose of the meeting is to get in the same corner. We are on each other's team and not opponents. If you are a Christian, pray together before the meeting starts, and ask God to allow you to communicate with compassion and with the goal of improving your marriage through the meeting.

Watch Your Marriage Grow

We hope you'll find this weekly meeting as helpful as we have. We've practiced *The Marriage Meeting* from the beginning of our marriage and have missed only one or two weeks. While every marriage has challenges, we have found we very rarely fight (almost never). That is not to brag, because left to our own devices, we would. The lack of fights is largely due to the fact that our communication is strengthened through the meeting.

Leading out in the meeting is a great avenue for me to express to Amy the importance of investing in our marriage. I take the initiative to launch this special time each week.

Husbands, I challenge you to invest in your marriage. This is a straightforward way to do so.

We want you to experience intimacy in your marriage. It is the reason this guide is short, so that even "non-readers" can use it. We hope your meeting times help you as much as they have helped us.

Get Connected

For more tips on meetings, additional questions, and other marriage insights, visit TheMarriageMeeting.com.

Also join the conversation on our Facebook page @TheMarriageMeeting. We'd love to hear your experiences, additional questions you've added, challenges you've faced, or other insights.

Acknowledgements

We want to thank Cris and April Taylor for the insight they provided to us in our pre-marital counseling. Without their challenge, *The Marriage Meeting* would have never come to fruition.

CPSIA information can be obtained
at www.ICGtesting.com
Printed in the USA
BVHW042138310122
627717BV00020B/408